ANIMAL ADVENTURES

CRAZY CREATURES

Edited By Jenni Harrison

First published in Great Britain in 2019 by:

Young Writers
Remus House
Coltsfoot Drive
Peterborough
PE2 9BF
Telephone: 01733 890066
Website: www.youngwriters.co.uk

Book Design by Camilla Vidot

Softback ISBN 978-1-83928-517-2
Hardback ISBN 978-1-83928-518-9
Printed and bound in the UK by BookPrintingUK
Website: www.bookprintinguk.com
YB0425H

FOREWORD

I was delighted when I found out we were running this competition. Why? Because I knew that it was the **purr**fect theme for young writers to get their teeth (and claws!) into to create everything from heartfelt homages to **a-moo-zing** anecdotes! And I was right!

Poetry inspired by pets and the animal kingdom has always been one of our most popular topics, and this time was no exception. I had a **whale** of a time reading these wonderful entries that describe the young writers' love and devotion for all creatures great and small. Through their words I learned of their love for animals at home and their awe for those from far away too. The slimiest slitherers, the creepiest crawlers and furriest friends are all brought to life in these pages using a great combination of poetic techniques and imagination.

I promise you, if you love everything from amazing pets to fantastic beasts - this is where you'll find them!

Okay, enough of my animal puns, I'll stop now and let you start your journey through these animal adventures. Enjoy, they're **udderly** brilliant! (Oops!)

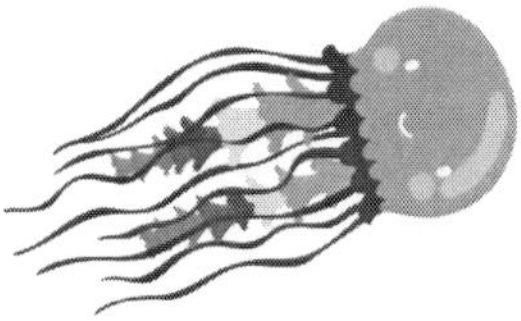

CONTENTS

THE POEMS

Elephants Are Big

E lephants can reach up to 3m tall,
L arge ears are what they are known well for,
E lephants are very sensitive,
P layful elephants are unharmful to humans,
H orns on elephants are called tusks
A sian elephants have really long teeth,
N early 80% of an elephant's day is spent feeding,
T usks are made out of ivory,
S kin on an elephant can weigh up to 200 pounds or over 900kg,

A ll elephant are mammals and are warm-blooded,
R ain helps elephants have fun and enjoy themselves,
E lephants are extraordinary and incredible,

B aby elephants weigh 200 to 268 pounds,
I love elephants because they are so loyal and loving,
G rey and dusty, but a kind-hearted and friendly mammal!

Anna Elizabeth Sijan (10)

Two Of A Kind

There is a creature by the hill and river,
In the cold Scottish breeze that will give you a shiver.
Under the stretched cloudy cyan-blue sky,
And above the family of moles who are very shy.

This wonderful creature is so alone,
In his monstrous cave made of rock and stone.
He goes to the ferocious river to catch bugs and fish for his every meal,
People don't even know he is real...

Enzo is the name of this unbelievable creature,
His vast purple decorated wings are his best feature.
He is a scaly plum dragon that has dark beady eyes,
And every single day he flies.

He glides through the sky in the rain or sun,
Ducking and diving is very fun.
The sky seems endless and the clouds are light,
And the small shining stars at evening are just a sight.

His big friendly smile is crowded with teeth so
pointy and great,
But all he really wants is a fun caring mate.
Enzo's nostrils are like marbles you get out a store,
And his strong throat can do a deadly intense roar.

His slippery scaly tail looked like it never ended,
His tail is so thick and extended.
His claws are so sharp like a nail,
He is so strong he could carry a baby whale.

When he walks it is like an earthquake,
The towering green trees and ground all shake.
Every animal and creature stayed away from this
one of a kind,
But what happened to lonely Enzo would make you
blow your mind.

One nippy day so cold and dry,
Enzo was bored so he went off to fly.
He launched off into the cool fresh air,
Just hoping animals won't shout or stare.

But he was feeling different and carefree,
Wanting something new to see.

He was fed up with his safe normal way,
So, he decides to fly far, far, away.

Instead of an east he took a west,
In the bushy tree past the bird's nest.
Speeding and speeding as fast as he can go,
Going down more and more low.

He slumped back down to the ground,
Which made an enormous pound.
Sat by a bush, puffing and taking a rest,
Thinking to himself, *I tried my best*.

He struggled back up on his giant paws,
Feeling as chubby as Santa Claus.
In a blink the silence broke,
It was like a creature woke...

It was a loud deafening cry,
Enzo stretched out his amazingly long neck to spy.
The wide nostrils and dark beady eyes,
This is the best surprise...

It was a beautiful dragon lying down,
So sad with a miserable frown.

The long black eyelashes complimenting her lovely face,
He could only peek but he wanted to know this grace.

He softly clambered over the brick and mossy wall,
He was petrified if he was to fall.
He started to slip and slide,
His fear was becoming more difficult to hide.

He was just hanging by a thread,
Bad thoughts going through his head.
His heart is beating uncontrollably fast,
This breath could be his last.

He shut his eyes ready to drop,
Because he was at the tippy top.
But in a blink, someone saved this beast,
It is who you would think least...

Enzo felt sharp hooks digging in his scales,
He heard a shushing noise as he wails.
He is lowered down by the pretty petite flowers,
Opens one beady eye, and an orange female dragon towers.

It was a neon orange dragon flaring her broad nostrils,
Her empathic big smile brightened up the hills,
Enzo just gave a confused grin,
He didn't know that an amazing life is going to begin.

The gorgeous creature pulled Enzo up onto his chubby paws,
Pronouncing that they both have super sharp claws.
She started to introduce herself in a sweet way,
"My name is Bo, please stay."

They started to stroll through the bushy wavy grass,
She started to talk about the chirping birds and plants like a nature class.
Enzo gathered up his confidence to talk to this female,
He presented himself while going all pale,

"I am Enzo and I live near the green hill,
And the long sapphire river that is so calm and still.

I had no idea there were lonely dragons here like me,
I love this beautiful attractive creature I see."

They chattered and shared all through the day,
They had more fun than a lifetime holiday.
And at the bright romantic dusk Bo said something unreal,
"Can we stay together forever to make our lives surreal?"

They chirped each other on the scaly neck as they held tight,
Hugged and snuggled all through the night.
One year later they had bonnie twins Link and Lilly,
They are a happy super family.

Emily Carson (11)

Grizzly Bear

I saw a grizzly bear today we walked into the wood
He scratched his claws upon my bed and yawned as it felt good
I combed his fur so tangly, brown and puffy
But as I used my hairdryer it made it warm soft and fluffy

I opened the door and we went outside
We went into the garden to play on our slide
Mum brought us two milky cups of tea
One for grizzly and one for me

After an hour we opened the gate
We went into the wood to investigate
I rode on his back and we went to see
If we could find a home for grizzly

The long trees were covered with bumpy bark
In the woods it was so very dark
After a while it started to rain
As I thought to myself, "Oh what a pain."

I got off of grizzly's back

And reached inside for my pakamac
We carried on all alone
To find my bear friend a wonderful home

Me and grizzly were very cold
As my pakamac was seven years old
We saw bushes and leaves and trees galore
But would we find grizzly a home? I wasn't sure

We saw families of birds nesting in their nests
But sticks came flying out when the wind blew from the west
We saw hedgehogs hiding in the leaves
And loads of flowers meant lots of bees

Then we saw an orange fox
His bushy tail as soft as socks
Loads of wildlife live in the woods
But we had to find grizzly a home as soon as we could

I soon wondered if we should go as it was getting late
I'm not a quitter though so we carried on through the gate

Grizzly roared for the one hundredth time
I don't understand bear language so he just had to mime

I followed him into a cave as dark and black as coal
I filled up with sorrow as I may not see my bear friend tomorrow
We investigated the cave me and him together
I knew I would remember my grizzly friend forever

But before I could finish my goodbye
A huge bear caught my eye
He roared as if to say thank you
He gave me a lick on the face too

You see the huge bear was grizzly's mum
And then I knew my work here was done
I sat outside playing with a stick on the ground
Maybe just maybe I would see grizzly around.

Ellie Lonergan (8)

Hippocrocopig

H is head like a hippo with a huge mouth and sharp teeth
I ts body is scaly and rough like a crocodile
P iggy tail that curls
P eeking out of the water waiting for animals to come
O n the bank of the waterhole he spies a herd of antelopes
C arefully he swims to the shore trying not to splash
R apidly the antelopes run away, petrified he's going to eat them
O h bother! Furious and frustrated he lets out an almighty grunt
C limbing out of the water, feeling lonely and sad, he nibbles the grass
O h my! He is a herbivore!
P oor thing, all he wants is some friends.
I n no time at all the elephants and rhinos come to play in the waterhole
G reat fun they have splashing each other with water and rolling in mud!

Harry Ayres (7)

If I Ruled The World

If I ruled the world,
I would stop all of the companies that are putting palm oil in our lovely things like mince pies
And I am about to explain why.
Did you know that there are just 6,300 orangutans left on Earth or a number that is near,
And it is estimated that 1,000 orangutans are killed every year.
These are also living things just like we are,
But they get killed when humans order food from a bar.
All the orangutans will soon be extinct just because the rainforest is their kingdom.
Sadly, that has made them your innocent victim.
Burning fires were seen in the face from out of space.
The astronauts spotted and thought, *what's this? Earth, surely not!*
The trees are the lungs of the world and if we lose the trees, we will no longer be able to live
And I promise I am not telling a fib!
Before you cut the amazing trees, please just stop and think.

Take a look at all of the beautiful animals and living things,
And I dare you not to blink.
Instead, stop, look and think.
The rainforest has an empire of animals,
A wonderful place they call home,
Just like the ancients did with Rome.
Get a book from the shelf
And please realise you're also killing yourself.
You need to stop right away
Because we need the beautiful animals to stay.
So, love the trees and please don't slay.
You should stop and think of what you do
Because all of this is down to you.
Diseases spread, but you don't care
So long as it's not happening in your bed.
Just think for a minute and use your head.
For the orangutans becoming extinct the rest of us dread.
You need to stop cutting the trees
And being so mean, please.

Troy Dennis (8)

The Ostrich That Could Fly

The sun to the earth was like icing to a cake,
Leaving a glaze after it had just been baked.
On the plains of Africa, shaded in the sun,
Lay a newborn ostrich, named little Bruhn.
So small, so weak, she gradually opened her eyes,
The other ostriches saw her and just had to empathise.
Mummy ostrich protected her little one,
Whilst daddy ostrich made sure the pack had gone.
Her grey, silky feathers, right down to her mini toes,
Were covered in dust from the sandy land that had decomposed.
She tried to stand but her knees were too feeble,
With the help of her mum and dad she eventually was able
To stand on two feet, her parents flapped.
Once the day had gone, the dark night came,
All weary and worn-out they huddled together and whispered good night.

In the morning, when the pack awoke, the sun shone bright,
Bruhn said to all the ostriches, "Today I'm going to fly."
But they all just laughed and squawked, "Why, oh why?"
Bruhn ran to the tree followed by her parents,
Her dad said, "Don't listen to them, if you want to fly, you can."
Her mother agreed and cried, "Yes you can, Bruhn!"
So Bruhn thought and thought, took a deep breath and ran,
She said, "I can do this, I'm Bruhn the flying ostrich! I can!"
Whoosh! "I'm flying!"
Moral: If you believe in yourself, you can do anything.

Jasminder Heer (10)

My Best Friend, The Hedgehog

One dark night
While swinging on the hammock
I heard a gentle rustle in the garden
And the dark green leaves moved
As if something was there.
I got up to have a look
And perched myself next to it.
Hunched over the moving leaves
I put my hand closer, investigating.
Then something touched my finger,
It was black and white,
Thin and narrow,
Hard and stiff,
And very, very spiky.
Then a leg popped out
And a head looked up at me while I gasped into the darkness.
I noticed it was a hedgehog
One like I'd never seen before.
Offering it some dog food, it devoured it rapidly,

Actually taking it from my hand and eating it next to me.
The next day, I spotted him again
And when he saw me, he started licking my hand.
The days passed like this
Until one dismal Tuesday,
When I had a genius idea.
I took him inside and found a cage
With water, food and a bed.
I played with him every day,
Throwing him in the air and catching him again.
I fiddled with his spikes, giving him a massage,
I turned him upside down, just for the fun of it.
We had fun together
And now I miss him,
Even more when I realise what I've done.
Indeed, he was a great friend,
But he belonged out in the wild.

Vasilina-Natalie Kutsinova (11)

Lone Wolf

As I made my way through the gnarled wood,
The sturdy ground turned to mud,
A creature resting in the fading sunlight,
Would wake and hunt soon,
With eyes as black as the starry night,
And a thick coat like the silvery moon,
The sky filled with ink,
Made the creature wake and blink,
It rose and approached me,
With apprehension I could see,
Noticing me as a friend he bowed,
He howled to the moon very loud,
And I followed him.
He was alone in his adventure in the night,
I was his shadow,
He climbed up onto a ledge with ease,
We stood in the cool midnight breeze,
Below us the town slept,
Peaceful and quiet.
He watched and waited, the hunt had begun,
Hazard filled the air with a chill,

He prowled slowly in the shadows,
A flash of teeth, a burst of speed,
The chase was over before I could take heed,
I felt nervous until, his gaze softened,
The wolf bowed his head again,
Presenting me with the gift he had caught,
I felt trust from then,
I put my hand upon his coat of silver,
The softness embraced me like a dream,
As unrealistic as it may seem,
I never wanted this night to end,
I peered into the eyes of my new-found friend,
He sighs,
Watching his breath form twisted phantoms,
While down below us the town lit their lanterns,
At the crack of dawn,
As I began to yawn,
We made our way back and said goodbye.

Ciar-Rose Astley (10)

Pirate Poppy And The Guinea Pigs

Pirate Poppy was a one-eyed dog,
She led a ship out to sea.
The Popeye it was called,
A fierce crew she had, though cute they may appear.

For guinea pigs they were,
Nibbles was the youngest who liked to eat all day.
Then came Duke who had quite crazy hair,
Last was Madam Crackers Bumblebut who had bee stripes near her rear.

Pirate Poppy seemed just about as tough as a carrot,
But she's softer than mash.
So what will happen when the wild cats attack?
Will the pigs save the day?

The wild cats leapt on board The Popeye,
"Arrr give us ya gold!"
Pirate Poppy was startled as she had no gold to give,

The wild cats saw this by the look on her face.

They huddled together efficiently. "Well we can't just leave."
Pirate Poppy stood frozen, wondering where the pigs were.
Truth be told they'd had too much lettuce and were out cold.
"We've come to a conclusion," the wild cats announced, "we'll just have your eye instead."

Now that's the tale of how my dog lost her eye,
To some fierce old cats.
The story was inspired by the name we call her now,
Pirate Poppy came from the fact she has one eye.

Layla Paige Oliver

Tigzy And Teeny

As tiny kittens, you were the size of apples,
Learning new things you would have to tackle.
At just ten days old,
You were both found outside in the cold,
In a dirty old skip,
Destined for the tip,
You got bottle feeds every few hours,
Each one you had you would both devour,
Being affectionate and getting strong,
At our home, where you now both belong
A long life full of love and care,
for our funny, crazy pair.
At the age of 12½,
Teeny got ill,
She couldn't be cured, even with pills.
Teeny passed away a few weeks later,
She was sick with kidney failure.
Three weeks in and then we find,
How this world can be so unkind,
As Tigzy's sick too,
She has the exact same thing.

The day she gained her angel wings,
Down to the beach,
Set off balloons to the sky,
The day we said our final goodbye,
To Tigzy and Teeny,
Our beautiful cats,
Together in Heaven, sisters back together,
Our memories of you we will treasure.
RIP Tigz and Teen,
They both passed away in 2017.

Kathryn Blades (11)

The Mysterious Animal

I went to the zoo and saw some animals but there was one that was very mysterious,
It was big, large and gigantic,
Was it real?
It was brown, furry and silky,
Was it real?
It had tusks as long as a car,
Was it real?
I could hear, smell, taste, touch and see it,
Was it real?
It was small, soft and nice,
Was it real?
It was trustful, loveable and bright,
Was it real?
It was cute, cuddly and young,
Was it real?
It was sweet, brave and funny,
Was it real?
It was creative, artistic and hyper,
Was it real?
It was vicious, precious and kind,

Was it real?
It was happy, snuggly and fast,
Was it real?
Adventurous, playful and strong,
Was it real?
It had eyes as big as a TV screen, it was as sweet as a lollipop and it had a mighty roar,
Was it real?
It was fierce, fast and furious,
Was it real?
It was fluffy, soft and sweet,
Was it real?
It was loud, dirty and as extinct as a dinosaur,
Was it real?
I could hug it, love it and ride it,
Was it a woolly mammoth?
I said, "Is it a woolly mammoth?"
I never said it was a woolly mammoth,
I mean it could be a Mastodon
So the adventure carries on.

Daphne Ogunkoya

Fire Lions

Fire lions are majestic,
They are powerful and energetic.
Every day they bring morning,
They also emit our Earth's warming.
They help us every single day,
By bringing light to our way.
They help us all the time,
If we demolish them, it will be a huge crime.

Their eyes burn stars' fuel,
Their eyes look like scorching pools.
Fire and light do they produce,
It is let out in an orange liquid juice.
Rays of gold silhouettes drift from their land,
Elegant manes of them give them a helping hand.

Of these mysterious creatures are knowledge ends here,
And because of our pollution they might disappear.
It isn't just these animals under threat,
In fact all animals from wild to pet.

Help to stop our polluting,
And assist these creatures by pollution stopping.
Every creature helps us every day,
And we must help in every way.

Now we must bid farewell,
And head back to Earth with my little spell.
Did you find the acrostic word 'fire'?
If you did your eye must be tired.
Say goodbye to this mystical land,
And I hope one day, of these animals we'll
understand.

Tvisha Lakshmeesh (10)

There's A Tiger In My Wardrobe

There's a tiger in my wardrobe,
Who protects me from those who come close.
There's a tiger in my wardrobe,
Who plays with me when I'm alone.

There's a tiger in my wardrobe,
Who gives me a cuddle when I am sad.
There's a tiger in my wardrobe,
Who gives advice to me when I feel bad.

There's a tiger in my wardrobe,
Who helps me climb up trees.
There's a tiger in my wardrobe,
Who looks over me when I'm asleep.

There's a tiger in my wardrobe,
Who protects me from the dangers.
There's a tiger in my wardrobe,
Who keeps me away from the strangers.

There's a tiger in my wardrobe,
Who helps me perfect my roar,

There's a tiger in my wardrobe,
Who taught me to pounce and soar.

There's a tiger in my wardrobe,
Who is my own fluffy guardian,
There's a tiger in my wardrobe,
Who helps me decorate the garden,

There's a tiger in my wardrobe,
Who has the mightiest laugh.
There's a tiger in my wardrobe,
Who is always on my behalf.

There's a tiger in my wardrobe,
And this tiger is very special to me.

Harrison Darwin (9)

Secret Life Of A Cat

I laze in your comfy bed,
Making it my own.
And when you are away,
I'm at home, all alone
Do I like to hunt mice, birds or fish?
The answer is unknown.
And when you start to gossip on your so-called smartphone.
You suddenly forget all about me so I start to moan.

I sneakily stroll around the food bowl,
Checking what's there.
If there's something fishy,
I look at you and stare.

You give me some food,
And then I head to the loo.
Then you walk in, holding your nose,
I glare at your scoop.
Why are you coming with those!
I'm doing my business!

Don't intrude!
Why are you?

You step on my tail, and I hiss and growl.
I start to avoid you, and then you make a scowl.
You place me on your lap,
And I perform my sleeping pose.
I take a tiny nap,
And wake up at your toes!

I curl near the heater,
Warming my cold paws.
I stretch on the scratch post,
Sharpening my claws.
You see a mouse and shriek and run.
I act as the hero, and chase it till I'm done!

I'm so cute and adorable with my fur.
You stroke my small head,
I close my eyes and purr.

Lyba Din (11)

Dobby

In his early life he loved to play
Out in the sun every day.
In the winter he would play in the snow
All fluffy and white like a marshmallow.
As he got older he was taught to do tricks,
From sitting down to fetching sticks.
He loved to go for walks in the woods, at the beach and in the park,
Where he would gallop around, happy as a lark.
Many years later, he started to go grey,
And wasn't as energetic anymore.
He would peacefully sit by the fire as I stroked his velvet ears
Although he was old, he still loved chasing balls which we would throw in the park.
He loved pigs' ears, a doggy treat
Which he would take to his bed to sit and eat.
He had silky, black fur as soft as a blanket,
And gentle brown eyes which looked kindly at you.
As his grand old age his hearing wasn't good,
He didn't bark at the doorbell like he usually would.

But his sense of smell was exactly the same,
And he'd sniff a lamp post for as long as he could.

Lily Beales

Sea Creatures

River is a merman bold.
He would sit and sing the whole of the day.
He would fill the sea-halls with a voice of power.
However, at night he would roam abroad.
And play with Melody.
In and out of the rock bridges.
And dressing her with sea-flower.

While holding her hair back with flowing locks.
They would play all night until their energy has drowned.
Melody is her name.
Her brilliance shines as she races River.
She possesses girlish qualities.
With womanly depth of understanding.

And the wisdom of the oldest souls.
She explores but her curiosity is never satisfied.
She is protected by River who truly loves her.
Her silliness is laced with sadness.
Her crystal-like eyes shine with child-like delight.
She has a smile that is uncertain.

However, a laugh that is heart-filled and whole.

She is a beauty of unworldly measure.
They have raven hearts, two silly mer souls.
Meant to be loved, not meant to be controlled.
They reveal themselves only to the special and true.
Moreover even rarer are ones who truly understand her mystique.

Blessica D'Costa

All About Cats

I like cats
They catch big fat rats
And chew up people's hats
But those are domestic cats

I like big cats
Ones that don't catch rats
Oh no!
They catch buffalo!
Sometimes they catch antelope
Jumping down a slope
Or sometimes mountain goats
The ones with the soft furry throats

But what about lions?
Rolling around in dandelions
The males have big mighty manes
And the females make daisy chains

And what about cheetahs?
We can't forget those
We all know their biggest enemy, is the garden hose

They really hate it when their fur gets wet
But nobody really knows why yet
All I know is it makes them super upset

Oh dear, I have forgotten the panthers
They are black, and when I say black, I mean super black
Black at the front, black at the back
And that is all I know
I wonder if they like snow

And what about snow leopards?
How do I even start?
Well, they don't like strawberry tart
Even if it is shaped like a heart
They are also quite shy
And I think they like steak pie.

Kassandra Tserpelis (9)

African Forest Elephant

A frican forest elephant
F ree to run wild
R emarkably styled
I t's got gorgeous detail
C arved like a stone, its colour is pale
A ll full of might
N early three metres in height

F ascinating and sometimes undutiful
O verwhelming and beautiful
R adiantly, it strides through the trees
E xhilarating to see
S maller than others, but a big personality
T he poachers are hunting, is there any
hospitality?

E ars are more round, tusks are more straight
L ives are going because of poachers' hate!
E lephants are beautiful and are majestic
P eople are hunting them, they are ballistic!
H unted only for the ivory tusk

A ll the more after dusk
N ot any elephant should be harmed!
T he elephants should instead be charmed.

Rose Raggett

My Favourite Animal Riddle

These soft-furred animals
Love climbing trees
But they don't go to carnivals
Dressed up as bees.

You see, if they dressed up as those black and yellow insects,
they would need to paint the white bits of their fur yellow
And although you couldn't catch them with nets,
The paint would itch and fill their hearts with sorrow.

Their ears are soft like a velvety plum
But don't mistake them for teddy bears.
Although nothing is smoother than their tum
You wouldn't want to be trapped in one of their lairs.

Please protect these animals because they are endangered,
One of the biggest threats is deforestation.

Bamboo is getting broken and destroyed,
Two other problems are poaching and pollution

My favourite animal needs helping,
They live extremely far.
These greedy herbivores spend most of their time eating,
Will you guess who they are?

Celeste Fodor-Magnen

The Flypan

The Flypan is the most magnificent creature on Earth,
It doesn't like to surf.
A Flypan has a wonderful gold horn on its head,
In freezing, cold winter it loves to go to warm, cosy bed.

The Flypan has large, pink, sparkly wings,
It loves to jump high like it has bouncy springs.
A Flypan is basically a panda with wings and a horn,
However, it is not a mythical unicorn.

The Flypan will slowly walk on four legs in spring,
It's really good at calm singing.
In autumn you will see the Flypan carefully preparing,
Its full harvest - it loves to do kind sharing.

The Flypan has quite a big diet,
So these are some things you've got to keep quiet:
You see the Flypan eats lots of delicious rainbow bamboo,

Which makes it go poop, poop, poop, poop, poop

The Flypan has a huge, fluffy belly,
Which makes it do burps that a really quite smelly

I love the Flypan
They don't get a tan.
I made up this beautiful creature,
I just love its features.

Amelie Ramdeen (8)

Robust Rhinos

Rhinos are wonderful creatures.
As animals, they have lots of interesting features.
They have a huge, sharp horn.
Of which in the past, many humans have torn.
They like to stomp about and are very large.
Look after yourself as at you they might charge.
Their little babies are really cute.
But their numbers are declining as they are the ones we like to shoot.
For the horn's medicine they are hunted down.
When they go to the waterhole for a drink, that's when the hunters are around.
Although they sound quite scary, they only ever eat plants and are gentle giants.
When they see humans, they get scared and charge at them like tyrants.
Currently though, rhinos are being shot.
Their horns are taken and their bodies are left to rot.
We need to help these wonderful things.
Otherwise, they will become as rare as diamond rings.

Humans have been hunting rhinos for far too long.
If you think they are boring, then you are
completely wrong.

Anika Gulati (8)

Eggo

This is an Eggo
A bit like a stego
He eats leaves and that's that
He's not short or skinny but tall and fat

He sits on the grass
And yells finally at last
But oh no it's not over
He's already met a Mars rover

Off he goes in a rocket ship
And yells, "This is lit!"
He was the first stego to step on the moon
Then he flies to Mars with a very fast zoom

He sits on the crumbly floor
And notices a bright light and a big shiny door
The bright light suddenly became dim
He sees an alien and UFO standing before him...

Don't think this poem is done
As how do you know if Eggo won?

Eggo will only rest
When he's finished his quest.

The UFO flew through space
At the very fastest pace
Earth was there just as far for Eggo to see
He was back just in time for tea.

Elise Charlotte Perry (10)

Bella-The-Boasting-Bird's Adventure

Bella was a most extravagant bird
She would sit in a tree for her words to be heard,
"Aren't I the most colourful bird there's ever been?"
"No," said Giraffe, "a better one I've seen."

"Where do they live?" Bella demanded.
"In a rainforest, one that's enchanted."
So the next morning, when it was light,
Bella flew away from the animals' sights.

She flew to a rainforest,
Full of evergreen trees,
Bursting with butterflies,
Lots of vines and reeds.

Then at that moment,
Bella heard a lovely, sweet song.
And realised she had always been wrong.

For there sat a parrot,
As colourful as can be.

"It really is the best bird I will
Have ever seen."

"But Giraffe said the rainforest was magic!
I must be in the wrong place! This is tragic!"
And then Bella thought,
Magic is here, all sorts.

Elodie Samantha Toms (10)

Why Quails Eat Snails

All the animals were on Noah's ark
All the animals, even the quail...
Except one, the male snail.
(The female ones were on the boat)
At last, Noah untied the rope
All the animals moved with the boat
The male snail was left alone
But it didn't even moan
It found a stick on dry land and clung on
He didn't know what was going on
But he wasn't dumb
He clung on until his body was numb.
After the boat came in Noah said,
"Goodness gracious we left the male snail!"
And as the animals were led
He passed out
For the snail wasn't dead
It was alive!
When Noah revived he said with a shout,
"Three cheers for the male snail!"
Everyone cheered apart from the quail

He was green with envy
And that's why quails eat snails!

Enana Aleismy (9)

The Tyrant

Once there was a tyrant which was hated least
Which came from the Middle East.
The toy got covered in yeast,
And the baking hot weather made a beast.

The thing became larger and grew and grew,
Until the whole Earth dropped all its dew,
And cows could no longer even say moo!
The world shook as everyone ran, when the thing whispered, "Boo!"

The tragic news spread,
Unfortunately a couple already dead,
And survivors fled.
It was worse than the plague with crosses red.

As the dreadful, fading days went by,
Every living cell at once made a sigh:
"Oh we're all going to die."
I wish I couldn't see with my eye.

The thing extinguished the last remaining
Labrador,
This was only the beginning of the next World War.
Even the children couldn't go to the local candy
store!
The devil was given a name... a 'dinosaur'!

Jack Hei Lee (10)

The Koala!

Hello, I'm sleepy. What's your name?
That's where I really get the fame!

I'm not the biggest fan of the ground
But if I'm there you have to not make a sound.

I climb slowly down but quickly if I see
A hungry dingo staring at me.

Living in the outback quiet, big, wide place
Maybe if I'm lucky I could fly to space!

I'd stare down at my mighty eucalyptus tree
Sipping a nice, warm cup of tea.

I'd go to Venus, I've heard it's hot
But that doesn't bother me a lot.

But maybe I'd get a little bit bored up there
So I'd fly back down to my nice, cool lair.

I don't get sunburnt because of my fur
Aussie is the best! I'm sure!

Yawn! I've been talking for ages!
You see, I go to bed in very complicated stages.

Goodbye for now, it's bedtime,
I hope you enjoyed the koala rhyme!

Amy Brogan (10)

The Pink River Dolphin

Did you know that there's a dolphin that's pink
Don't just stare, you better start to blink.

You really didn't know that? Oh my!
I mean it now, this is not a lie.

Who just asked if it's better than a horse?
Oh come on... it's a dolphin. Of course!

We all call our one Don
He is from the Amazon.

To be more specific from Brazil,
Doing barbecue is his skill
So make sure he's in charge of the grill.

Once when we were with this special dolphin
We heard someone calling him

It was his friend, that dear penguin
His name was Robin

Then Don said...

"You little penguin, so sweet not sour
Who can swim up to twenty miles an hour.

How I love the funny way you stand
When you start waddling your way across land.

We need to go now; we like to have late evening swims
So that's our goodbye from us dolphins!"

Annie Cadete (10)

A Snail's Life

You might be a human
And think I'm very bad
But, hey, I can hear you
And that makes me sad.
Lots of little birdies
Eat me and feel glad
But a bad reputation
Makes me feel mad.
You pick me up
And weee!!! I'm flying
Above the hedges
Oh no, I'm dying.
Why do you do this?
You might hear me plead
Yes, I eat your cabbages
But I also eat your weeds!
So I think you will find
That you need to say sorry
And don't throw me in the road
Or I'll get crushed by a lorry!
I really am a helpful soul

I just don't understand
I'm only trying to survive here!
Why throw me off your land?
Next time you see a snail,
Do not harm it please!
It'll be doing what comes naturally
Like eating up your weeds!
If I eat your precious plants,
I do apologise
I do not really mean to,
Perhaps they're in disguise

Megan Waghorn (12)

Blobfish

In tough times
With sad minds
I will help you find
Your purpose in life
And to make you understand
You could be as small as a mouse
Or as big as an elephant
You're just as significant.

If you think you're all alone
And that no one feels the same
Then look around you
You're not alone
They feel the same
Even if you have fame
It doesn't mean they are happy
It could be an act.

Now let's get to the roots
Before this sadness shoots
People care about you
They can help you through

You don't have to stay still
Because you may find
That people love you
Just like I do.

Never change
You're perfect the way you are
I love you blobfish
Never forget it.

Alex Johns (14)

Venom Claw

A beast with a tail and a leg for a nose,
An arm so red like a freshly grown rose.
Spikes on its back with whiskers so fine,
Extremely sharp claws and three eyes in a line.

A juxtaposition from its ragged brown fur,
Is its speed as it dashes around in a blur,
A beast so broad, fierce and complicated,
Has such a fiery tongue to leave you frustrated.

Stalking its prey in the deep undergrowth,
Conjuring up lies and unfaithful oaths,
To get its own way and its deep desires,
Never backs down and never tires.

This confusing specimen is truly one of a kind,
And indeed it was a seldom find,
The personality of this beast lives up to its name,
Venom Claw I named it, as it vanished in a flame.

Kiri Jane Hobbs

An Old Warhorse

For decades I have been trotting sagely on the barren grounds of war,
This performance of mine being repeated encore,
With riders of different mode - some steering with full speed,
Others not even bothering to take heed.
My red roan coat once tinged with chrome green,
Now black blemishes and scars etched deep, left to be seen.
I used to canter freely in the undulating green pasture,
My powerful hooves propelling faster
Until the deafening roars of gunshots shadowed the sky,
Bringing a veil of darkness and a life-long cry.
Caged by wooden fences: no longer free, no longer needed,
Faltering legs and wincing eyes, yet my wounds unheeded.
The stench of death lingering near, now deprived of my sanity
If only this sonnet of a poor mare could rekindle their humanity.

Rameen Masood (16)

The Mouse

Mouse!
What's that noise?
I heard something, I know I did.
A kind of scratch-scurry-scrabble, coming from behind the fridge.
Oh no, it's a mouse! I can't stand mice.
In fact, I'm terrified of them.
Just thinking about them makes me shudder and if I see one I go crazy;
Scream, jump on the nearest chair, table, anything;
I don't care, just don't let it near me!
It's totally stupid, I know.
I mean, they're not exactly that ferocious. Are they?
It's not as if there is a crocodile or anything.
Argh! It's at the fridge!
If I try to catch it I would probably faint after touching it.
Right, I'm leaving.
Okay I'm in the garden now.

I suppose this all wouldn't be silly if I were a human,
But for crying out loud I'm a cat!

Ebunoluwa Temidara

The Panther

Panther, panther, dark knight
In the forest of the night.
He has eyes like balls of fire,
He climbs a tree to get much higher.

He sneaks up on his prey,
His fur is black and grey.
His teeth are sharper than knives,
He is a cat, he has nine lives.

He is nocturnal, he hunts at night,
If you see him you will get a big fright.
In the night the panther prowls,
Their steaming breath is very foul.

The panther is very evil and stealthy,
He has to eat to stay healthy.
The panther has sharp claws,
He also has powerful paws.

Panther, panther, dark knight,
In the forest of the night.

It has eyes like balls of fire,
He climbs the trees to get even higher.

William Evans (10)

The Love Of Hedgehogs

In the garden during the sunset
There was a prickly, spiky animal
Shuffling and sniffling
Seeing the worms to chew on.
Such a cutie to gaze.
Far too shy, not too bold.
Sniffing out the slimy worms.
Tiny and spiky; a lovely hedgehog.
Chewing on the slugs and snails.
To eliminate all their trails.
Just stealthily detecting them.
It is one of my favourite animals
Going through the leaves.
The spiky body has never been seen.
Seeking out a place to rest.
Somewhere to build a nice, cosy nest.
The springtime comes around once again.
The hedgehogs will come out to entertain.
Creeping around the garden path.
Such a joy to watch it go.

In amongst the flowerbeds.
Undercover at night.
The hedgehog is a wonderful sight.
Moving from log to log.
My precious, sweet hedgehog.

Habiba Begum (14)

Cheetah Cheetah

Cheetah, cheetah, on the go,
Always running, never slow.
In the wild full of heat,
You shoot like a bullet to go and eat.

Why did God make a creature so fast?
Then made animals that will always be last.
Such elegant fur, soft and fine,
In the sun so it can shine.

You have a quick-thinking brain,
With a paw to trip your prey.
With your long balancing tail,
You can run and never fail.

Who can be ever so graceful?
Also look ever so beautiful.
You are the most amazing creature,
With all your athletic features.

Cheetah, cheetah, on the go,
Always running, never slow.

In the wild full of heat,
You shoot like a bullet to go and eat.

Danielle Holzhausser (10)

My Cat, My Best Friend

Loads of people have pets,
Iguanas, hamsters, a cool set.
My pet is as bright as the sun,
He's cute, he's sweet
And a whole lot of fun.

I love to stroke his ginger fur
And quietly listen
To his soft, little purr.
His eyes look up and sparkle at me,
As he drinks his milk
And I drink my tea.

The day I met him,
He sat on my lap,
Curled up and snuggled,
Ready to nap.
His green eyes twinkled away
Reminding me of how much I love him
In every single way.

Then I just realise
This kitten doesn't seem to have any mittens,

So I knit him a special pair,
Just to simply show
How much I care.

Emily Agha Mohammad Zadeh (11)

William The Wicked Wolf

William has greasy matted brown fur
Horrible hypnotising eyes
Dagger-like yellow teeth
Claws as sharp as horns

One dark day an evil plan came into his brain
He thought his plan was genius
He would need an army to help him
He would go to the village

The nice people took one look at him and fainted with shock
When they woke they saw his horrible hypnotic eyes staring into theirs
They were hypnotised
He had lots of evil servants to help him to defeat the worst enemy of his life

With his evil gang he went to war with Wally the Woodcutter
Wally was an utter nutter
William and his gang tried to defeat him

But it was no use
They lost
The spell was broken
William the wicked wolf was no more
He was never seen again.

Katie Thornton (6)

Super Pandas

P andas are furry
A nd they are like cuddly bears
N ext to a panda would be bamboo so if they get hungry, they can eat it
D o you like pandas? I love pandas as they are one of my favourite animals
A nd pandas live in China
S o giant pandas live up to 20 years old

A nd pandas are black and white
R eady pandas - get ready to climb. Pandas love to climb
E ating - pandas spend 14-16 hours a day eating bamboo

C uteness - pandas are so cute
U p in the mountains of Central China is where they live
T hese are facts about a panda's life
E yes of a panda are not that big.

Bella Rose Stewart (8)

Phoenix Fire

I fly on my red phoenix
Up, up, up over the clouds we swoop.
I am a wizard.
A person sees my phoenix shoot fire.
I'm on the news!
I look down at the fire-strewn cities beneath me as I fly away.
I feel the wind in my hair.
My phoenix lands in our home, the cave
Where its eggs are resting on the rocks.
I feed it its dinner (dead ferrets)
And have my own (fish and chips)
And lie down to sleep in my bed.
I think of the adventure I've had today
And how big the world around me is.
With these thoughts I drift off to sleep
And dream of riding my dragon for my next adventure,
Then wake up for a whole new day of exciting adventures.

Ella Hargreaves (7)

Rufus

I used to stumble on the pavement cracks,
Too close to passers by,
Each journey seems to take years when
It's me, myself and I.

But then I got my guardian angel,
Rufus, the name I chose,
He helps me everywhere I go,
So now my confidence grows.

When I hold on to his lead,
I feel like I'm in power,
I could conquer any path,
I could climb Everest in an hour!

Rufus shows me where to go,
By my side all the time,
He is now my very best friend,
And my partner in crime.

I may not be able to see the world,
But I see one thing clear as day,

My love for my guide dog Rufus
Is never going away!

Alannah Rose Marsden (15)

Lionheart

With noble pride and royalty
Strides the king of the jungle, the lion and his pride towing in loyalty

Ambling through the plains of Nsefu
Hunting away through the vast lands of Sasan Gir for food

Lionesses with eyes alert and cubs on trail
Hunting for food to provide the pride without fail

Cubs play fighting adorably
The size of a grown domestic cat approximately

Lions with manes that they so prize
And slanted brown, piercing eyes

Benevolent lionesses with hearts of gold
Letting nomadic cubs suckle even if they are unknown

Heads held high and the pride on their side
And bloodthirsty eyes looking for prey trying to hide

A symbol of nobility and courage
These brave lions have a diminishing occurrence.

Yaana Mishra (12)

Lost

Your amber eyes are warmth in the bitter wind as the snow blows athwart the night sky,
And your fur is sleek silver,
The gleaming canines that smile at the moon are dangerous but yet comforting to I,
In this time of loneliness.
Your song that echoes through the timber is poetry in its own right,
To which I deeply slumber,
And the northern sky is brilliantly lit with colours shining bright,
to watch over us as we go.
You are my saviour, my one and only companion, my friend,
Who guided me home tonight,
But as the town comes slowly into view our adventure must sadly end.
Safe in my own snug and tranquilising bed I hear you cry and smile,
Deep in satisfaction,
Glad to have walked with a wolf for a while.

Jordana Caitlin Hall

Pawsitively Bearilliant!

Polar bears, pandas, black bears and brown,
Have you ever seen one hanging upside down?

They come from all over, all around the globe,
Can you imagine seeing one in a fluffy robe?

Some enjoy bamboo, whilst others prefer seal,
How would you feel if you were a bear's evening meal?

Brown bears can run exceptionally fast,
If you dared to race one do you think you would come last?

Bear cubs climb trees, too high to be found,
Are mother bears impatient sat waiting on the ground?

Intimidating, strong, stealthy and tall,
Would your teacher be frightened if you brought one into school?

Cute, furry, playful, but with a ferocious bite,
My teddy is the only bear that I want to cuddle at night!

Maya Isabelle Tinn-Stephens (10)

Animal Adventures

Rising from the deep blue sea,
Beautiful but shy creatures emerge to be seen,
Their intelligent nature really shines through,
Helping each other to do things they want to do,
From when the sun sets to when it brightens,
The dolphins continue their journey full of excitement,
Their satisfying whistle getting others attention along the way,
Diving free in this wonderful day,
Chasing and throwing is what they do best,
As it is good to hunt and protect the rest,
They fill the ocean with calm, quiet sounds,
Their love and affection is all around,
There is nothing better for a dolphin to be,
Than in the deep blue sea.

Imethma Weerarathna

The Animal Journey

Snake, snake, slithering snake,
Eating all my birthday cake,
What a horrible mess you make!

Croc, croc, stuck under a rock,
Munching mud from on a block,
Giving people an enormous shock!

Shark, shark, lost in the park,
Getting scared of the dusty dark,
Crying when it hears a dog bark!

Fox, fox, chillin' in his box,
Painting patterns on his socks,
Stealing food from the docks!

Cow, cow, saying, *meow!*
Thinking that it's a cat right now,
But that would be a wow!

Goat, goat, in a moat,
Setting sail in his milky boat,
In order to stay afloat!

Hattie Boxall (9)

Nothing But A Worm

I wish that I could be a dog
Who gets all the love and affection
But I'm nothing but a worm
Who never gets any attention

I wish I could be a monkey
Always making people cheery
But I'm nothing but a worm
Which makes me very teary

I wish I was a bird
Free to glide and soar
But I'm nothing but a worm
Who can never leave the floor

I wish to be a lion
Who bravely guards his land
But I'm nothing but a worm
Fearing where people will stand

I wish I was a fish
Swimming about in the sea

But I'm nothing but a worm
Always dreaming of what I want to be

But I am a worm
And that's all that I can be
So I must learn to love
Me for being me.

Isla Belle Williams (11)

Into The Unknown

Luna and Tess
Chasing a ball
Through fields and hedges

I said fields and hedges
Silhouetted against the setting sun
Every which way I turn
They are there

Luna Luna chasing
A butterfly
Into the unknown

Tess, Tess
Down by the stream
Under the canopy of swaying leaves

Oh Luna
I said oh Luna
Prancing about
Soaking me

We sit down under a maple tree
And eat

I set up my blue tent
Splattered with mud

We shan't be gone long
Into the unknown together

You are not alone
I said you are not alone.

Daisy Jane Wilkes (9)

Reborn From The Ashes

In the still of the night
Just before sunrise
A magnificent creature builds its nest
While humans lay their heads to rest
It carefully puts each branch
In place with laborious detail.
The tiredness of the creature truly evident
Though it does not take away from its beauty.
The sun starts to ascend
And the bird begins to stretch
Its feathers gleam a beautiful gold
It cranes its head back as it sings,
A soul-stirring melody that stops the sun.
An atom falls from the sky,
Igniting and extensive fire that consumes,
But don't fret, in three days
The phoenix will be back - born again.

Hadassah Awoliyi

I Had A Dream About Terrabi Cats

Terrabi cats eat dogs, tigers, lions, spider and mice
Most terrabi cats like to eat animals in stew
They boil their food in a shoe as hot as a brew
They dug a big tunnel maze
The wrong way does not lead to any terrabi cats
But the right way does
Sitting there is a terrabi cat as big as a giant
Of two different colours - soft skin and woolly white
Waiting for its food
Suddenly a dog reached the end of the maze
A cute, little, furry dog
The terrabi cat licked her lips hungrily
Thinking of the dog boiling in stew
Then
I woke up and realised
I had a dream about terrabi cats, phew!

Ayesha Ata-Ur-Rehman

Cat And Mouse

I love cats
But not mouse
There was a mouse that was fat
In my house
The mouse was fearless
In my little house
My mum's not careless
About the naughty mouse
John was screaming
"There's a mouse!"
So I started cleaning
The mouse out of my house
The mouse was looking for some food
So we started binning
Food for our own good
We started cleaning
The entire whole house
And I started binning
The naughty little mouse
Today is my first stage
Of being a cat

Next time I'll cage
More mice in the cages they're supposed to be at.

Enqi (Jack) Dai (10)

The Snow Leopard

The majestic snow leopard sits fixed,
Gazing out across the vast mountains,
Looking for a meal to feed its hungry cubs.

It spots a goat, separated from the herd,
And it stalks it with the advantage of high ground,
It sneaks up, camouflaged, then pounces.

Only just missing,
The chase begins,
The snow leopard sprints down the rocks,
Not slipping, determined,
Cornering its prey,
Strangles it to death with its razor-sharp fangs,
And drags the hefty carcass back to its den.

At least for the next few days,
The satisfied snow leopard won't go without food.

Harrison Lord (11)

My Dinosaur Poem

My name's Finley, I'm a dinosaur expert,
just stick with me and you won't get hurt.
Raptors are my favourite and they hunt as a pack,
to catch their enemy then suddenly attack!
Some dinosaurs lay lots of eggs,
they can be small or have long legs.
Spinosaurs have razor-sharp teeth to eat,
there are not many dinosaurs that they can't beat.
Pterodactyls live in the sky,
and can spot their prey from way up high.
A diplodocus is a herbivore,
they eat grass, trees, leaves and more.
T-rexes have the loudest roar,
they can eat a whole person and still want more!

Finley Collier (6)

Wolf

I found you.

You have no way of escaping me now.
You should probably give up.
And probably finally admit.
That you were wrong.

The thousands of people you could have upset.
Yet you had the luck.
Of it being me.
How sad.

It's no secret that my jaws are used to hurt.
To rip the damned embarrassment.
Of believing and trusting.
You.

My claws have already dug into the earth's flesh,
My muzzle has already been bloodied,
My eyes have already found you,
You can't escape me now.

To you, I must look crazy.
To others, I'm a wolf.

I'm chill with that.
Because

Because the wolf only needs enough luck to find you once.

Chloe Scott

I Am Just A Simple Honey Bee

I am just a simple honey bee
I work all day, I sleep all night
To human existence I dedicate my life
They work us to our deaths
Although they call our honey the best
It's just not good enough
They demand, they force
They trap us in their farms
Pollinate a third of our plants
Make my honey
They say,
They'd die without us
And soon we will too
For 30 million years, we have been a constant on this earth
Haven't we sustained them enough?
This is how they repay us?
When we become extinct, the humans will too
Now let's just see who's going to pollinate their food?

For I am just a simple honey bee
Who cares about me?

Chloe Jasmine Woodward (14)

The Phoenix

Soaring through the sky,
Flying through the clouds so high,
Like a shining hot-red sun,
A burning heatwave sure to come.

My phoenix is an elegant red flower,
Blossoming and growing every hour,
A blazing fire rapidly extending,
Growing and bending.

My phoenix is a tranquil nightlight to my fears,
Comforting me when I am in tears,
Bring me elation and joy,
Like a toddler receiving a brand-new toy.

My phoenix stays with me always,
Engulfing me with warm sunlight rays,
My phoenix is beautiful to see,
Yet the only person who sees him is me.

Tadiwa Nyemba (11)

Wolves

As sharp as daggers they were steel-grey claws
That extended from large, midnight-black paws.
Dark fur caught slivers of light as it stood
Like a majestic warrior, towering over the wood.

Ivory teeth menaced between its jaws,
Ears alert, looking for the noise's cause.
Squinting, inky eyes like a deep, gloomy pool,
Lips stained red from blotchy blood, dripping with drool.

Clever and strategic, cogs whirl in its brain,
Protectiveness for its loved ones drips off like rain,
It's always exalted inside and outside,
Always fit to lead and always fit to guide.

Amira Benning-Prince (11)

My Favourite Animal Is A Panda

My favourite animal's a panda,
They like to eat bamboo,
My favourite animal's a panda,
I hope you like them too!

My favourite animal's a koala,
They like to live in trees,
My favourite animal's a koala
Because they don't use keys!

My favourite animal's a tiger,
They're full of oranges and blacks,
My favourite animal's a tiger,
You won't see one in a sack!

My favourite animal's a snow leopard,
Because they are so cute,
My favourite animal's a snow leopard,
Because they play the flute!

Alys Madelyn Thomas (8)

King Of The Jungle

K ing of the animals
I t's the ruler of the land
N ot afraid of anything
G reat fear it gives the others

O nly with its own kind it is comfortable
F riends with its own

T he king of the jungle
H orrible rumours stir
E ating their own, some may say

J ealous, the others are
U nderneath their supposed bravery
N ever going to face their fear
G reat fear
L ions cause them
E veryone is afraid of the King of the Jungle.

Shania Miah

Animal Alphabet

As angry as an alligator,
As buzzy as a bee,
As cuddly as a cat,
As daft as a donkey.

As enormous as an elephant,
As giant as a giraffe,
As happy as a hedgehog,
As interesting as an iguana.

As jazzy as a jellyfish,
As keen as a kangaroo,
As mad as a monkey,
As natty as a newt.

As observant as an octopus,
As pretty as a peacock,
As quiet as a quokka,
As rapid as a raccoon.

As slow as a sloth,
As terrific as a turtle,
As unfaltering as an umbrellabird,

As vigilant as a vulture.

As wild as a wallaby,
As xenial as an x-ray tetra,
As youthful as a young yak,
As zany as a zebra.

Tamsin Lucy Wilcox (10)

Octopi

If you and I were octopi
Would we eat fish?
We probably would
If only we could
If you and I were octopi.

If you and I were octopi
Would we jiggle around?
We probably would
If only we could
If you and I were octopi.

If you and I were octopi
Would we have spots?
We probably would
If only we could
If you and I were octopi.

If you and I were octopi
Would we eat fish?
We probably would
If only we could
If you and I were octopi...

If you and I were octopi...
If you and I were octopi...

Josie Vince (6)

Which Animal Shall I Be?

Which animal shall I be?
If I could be any animal,
Any one at all,
I'd have to choose between hundreds of them,
And they can be big or small.

I could be an eagle, ruling the skies,
But there is one problem; the sky is full of flies!

Or maybe I could be a bee,
Collecting the sweet honey,
But if I'd have to be a bee,
I'd be too busy!

Or maybe I could be a cheetah,
Catching my prey fast,
Of speed I would be king,
But I don't think that's quite my thing!

So I've looked at all the choices,
And also all the extras,

But right now I will chant,
That I am still an ant!

Abdulaleem Hanoun (11)

Dear O' Deary Shark

Are you proud of your knife-like fins?
Do you think about your sins?

Why do you like the cold, dark waters?
Do you care about your slaughters?

Why do you put others in danger?
Or do you put them in a death chamber?

Why do you fake your glassy eyes?
And do you like the surprise?

Is stealth your approach or the big bang?
Why do humans take the prang?

Do you think your skin is tough?
Or is it not so rough?

Do you like your razor teeth?
And use them from beneath?
Dear o' deary shark.

Matthew Thomas (10)

The Life Of A Bee

Buzzing flower to flower,
Flying aimlessly through the sky.
People may be reluctant to admit,
There is more than meets the eye.
It holds the pollen close to its chest like a baby.
Its pride, passion, life - even more maybe.
Though there comes a time when life must end.
Sting. Buzzing. Silence.
But before this it must go through what we cannot comprehend.
Organs torn, it carries on - flower to flower.
Weaker and weaker.
Dead before too long.
The yellow for pollen and honey,
The black for sting and bulbous eyes.
These are the colours that represent,
The bee's striped line of life and death.

Xara Schieferstein

The Turteal

The turteal, half turtle, half seal, splashes in the sea,
Their favourite food to eat is fish, they chew it with glee.
The skin of them is extremely light grey,
And they are always looking for their prey.
The fish wish they were vegetarian,
You won't see them in an aquarium.
If you see one you'll be shocked
But they are nothing like an angry croc.
They live deep in the ocean,
So you will need a water-breathing potion.
Their shell is impossible to crack
Even if you give it a big smack.
No animal is better than the turteal!

Pippa Siddiky (8)

Worth A Try?

I miss my lovely home,
They took everything I own
I don't know what to do,
So I thought I'd lay my trust in you.

A giant claw demolished my ground,
I heard shrieks, a siren sound,
My family are all gone,
I've got no strength to carry on.

No trees to climb,
No food to eat,
Oh how I feel so weak,
I'm constantly frightened when I hear a creak.

But still I lay my faith in you
Question is, what will you do?
Protect my species
Keep me alive
Do you think it's worth a try?

Amilia Kate Burke (13)

Family

The sound of the low whistle as they drift off to sleep
The ferocious growl that can be heard when they're chasing with a leap
The softness of their fur for when they cuddle with their cubs
Cubs that are playing, pouncing and hiding down in the shrubs.

There are many families of this species, although they're being hunted down
Only because their fur is soft enough to be turned into a gown
But sometimes the families escape from poachers luckily just in time
For this is a family of wolves who sneaked into my rhyme...

Rosie Millington (11)

A Happy Dog

I'm a happy dog you see
If I had the glory to be
I would tell you all about me
I would like you all
To pass my ball
I'm a happy dog you see
If I had the power to be
I could control the world like you
I could wag my tail like mad
Then sit about feeling sad
I'm a happy dog you see
I run about catching a flea
When I moan
I eat a bone
Then I have a body full of energy
I'm a happy dog you see
My owner takes care of me
I get fed, put to bed
That is what my owner does for me.

Simran Shanan

Lion Lifesaver

He is royal
They call him king
Out of the bushes
He will spring
But he is not carnivorous
He eats fruit thrice
Respects all creatures
Including mice
The love in his heart
Is not given to thee
Humans of the carn
Especially he who eats meat
I found him that day
I smiled and waved
But I saw who
Was gonna be saved
He who eats meat
Was not very happy
He took me away
Gonna get snappy
But lion saved me

Meat-eater was beaten
He rescued my skin
Before I was eaten.

Alice Lough (9)

Like A Common Predator

See reflections on the water.
More than darkness in the depths.
See it move through smoke and mirrors.
Feel the presence in the crowd.
Tall and dark, like a predator,
Fast and cool.
Suave and smooth
And it can soothe you like vanilla.
Don't think of the danger or the stranger is gone
Looking for trouble,
The gentleman's a killer.
And you know it's going straight for your heart.
Like a knife cutting through life
Like every day's the last.
You drift through the years and life seems tame
A pity if it grieves them.
Like every day's the last.
He is no fool.

Jasper Teoh (15)

Birds

Squawk go my parrots,
Ding goes the bell.
What's that you say?
Birds talking to each other
Words that you may not want your kids to hear.
Playful animals.
They can turn nasty when they feel threatened.
The beautiful grey and red feathers expand as they fly.
Quadruple the noise.
Quadruple the fun.
You may hear them miles away.
Play football with them through the cage
Hear them learn new things.
Birds are the best animals to have
They may be messy, but nobody can beat their love for us.

Kelsey Rickard

Octo The Octopus

Octo is the best you know,
He can swim side to side like the tide
He's kind and friendly, generous and lovely.
His wide, warm smile can make others smile!

Octo is different to the others you know
'Cause unlike the others he has nine genius brains!
His matt black ink blinding the enemy
His fascinating skin camouflaging with his surroundings.

Octo's curly wurly tentacles dance about all day
Everyone admires his shining tentacles everywhere he goes
You never know, you might meet Octo you know...

Melis Akman (10)

The Joy Of A Dog

A different dog every day,
Black eyes or brown,
Brightens me anyways.
Spiky fur or hanging down,
Sparks a grin on my face.
Even melting away all your worries!

Naughty or docile,
Still makes fun glitter all around,
Especially in the costume of a crocodile.
They might cause trouble,
Like lying on the couch with muddy paws,
But, come on, just excuse the adorable.

Dogs are amazing,
Even intelligent (actually, a lot).
In glory and praise, brightly blazing,
That can fill more than ten pots.
You can express their level of breathtaking,
But that's okay if you cannot.

Debotri Basumatary (11)

Birds!

Oh, kestrel
Your call is orchestral!
Oh, robin
You are a-bobbing
Oh, kingfisher
How you fish a
Tasty snack to eat
Oh, thrush
You flush
The air with a coo and a song
Oh, starling
Protected under Mother's wing
Oh, kite
Take flight
Oh, owl
As you howl
In the night
Oh, tern
You'll learn
To get used to the cold
Oh, goose

You let loose
And express your anger!
Birds fascinate the human eye
Ascending to the azure sky
They soar aimlessly above the clouds
Creating V-shaped crowds
The wind propels upon their backs
Racing along in their packs.

Seth Radley Diaz (10)

Icy Claws

From the Arctic comes a sound,
On the ice-covered ground,
Cuddly, white, out of sight,
Sleeping in the frosty night.

In the snow it's very warm,
Even in the coldest storm,
A polar bear with sharp claws,
Nothing's quieter than his paws.

He's sneaking up on his prey,
He's hunting fish all day today,
He's using his black nose to smell the fish,
He's grabbing them up and licking his lips.

Sleeping in the cold snow,
As the wind does breathe and blow,
A polar bear with sharp claws,
Nothing's quieter than his paws.

Mujtaba Hussain

The Dragon

A darkness in the sky swallows up all living things,
"Everyone run!" I scream,
Like a terrible dream, Mother Nature has turned on us,
Then I watch as the fire devours all,
Our blood covers the sky, The dragon returns.

The dragon wasn't always this mean,
I think, he just wanted some peace,
Perhaps we woke him from his dream,
Or he has a hunger that failed to cease.

Whatever the reason,
When you come down to the deepest depths,
Step quietly, for you don't want to wake the dragon,
For you will see he is hungry for humans.

Katie Wilkinson (10)

Alphabetical Pets

Ants are small and strong
Birds fly
Cats are cute
Dogs are friendly
Elephant are huge
Foxes are sometimes orange
Giraffes are huge
Hamsters are tiny
Insects are tickly
Jellyfish sting
Kangaroos are good at jumping
Lions are scary
Monkeys are checky
Nighthawk is a bird
Octopus are orange
Penguin live in water and on ice
Rabbits have cute eyes
Spiders have eight legs
Tigers are loud
Umbrella birds have big heads
Vipers are snakes

Wasps sting you
Yellow baboon is a baboon but yellow
Zebras have black and white stripes

Amy Dryburgh

Funky Monkey

This is my poem about a monkey
I think it will be really funky
Monkeys make me laugh, they're so funny
I watched them in the zoo when it was sunny
They searched each other's fur for bugs
I even saw a baby one, it got lots of hugs
They ate all their food really fast
They always saved their bananas until last
They chased each other around all day
They have lots of fun when they play
I like the way they swing from the trees
Mummy... can I have a monkey please?

Skyler-Mai Wild (4)

A Meerkat Poem

Think of a meerkat - what does it do?
It scurries around and lives in a zoo.
Sensing danger, it looks up high,
Scanning for predators flying in the sky.

Where does it come from? What does it eat?
It lives in a burrow and munches on meat.
Posting a sentry, they bathe in the sun,
But when an alert is given, they run, run, run...

Are they a family? Are they a mob?
They're classed as a gang when they're out on the rob!
Cute and cuddly, their fans abound,
But go to southern Africa and they are found all around.

Phoebe Anna Heasman (9)

The Tiger Is The Beast Of The Night

The tiger is the beast of the night.
He roams through cities and gives a terrifying bite;
Cats and dogs watch as he chases a trespassing fox down the black, trashed streets...
His clumsy, soft, hairy, fluffy feet smell of different things combined, as he travels his way down to hell!
When he falls, he gets angry and roars his mighty evil song down the night; people run around, crazy with a fright.
His tail gives you a shiver and an earthquake will awake as he places it on the rough ground.
The shiver is a shocker!

Ellora-Ines Silvestre (9)

Bonnie

Her eyes are like melting chocolate
Eyelashes are like wire, protecting her way of seeing the world.
The sun plays peek-a-boo with the clouds as she watches in curiosity.
This is what makes Bonnie complete.

Her eyes are kind, determined and energised.
Nostrils sing out sighs of calmness and joy as the sun gallops higher into the sky.
Her ears dance around, picking up every sound.
What is it like to be a creature of such power?
That question will remain a secret.

Annabelle Woolveridge (13)

My Little Puppy

M y puppy, you are my best friend
Y ou are so nice

L ittle wiggly tail you have
I love spending time with you
T iny beautiful hairs
T winkling eyes you have
L ovely pet
E yes are full of kindness.

P uppy you are always helping me
U sually saving me from strangers
P uppy your eyes shine in the dark
P uppy you have sharp claws
Y ou are a perfect pet for me.

Nivethaa Kabilan Saivarajan (7)

Cats And Dogs

Cats and dogs are an unwise combination
When they're together there's always complication
You must not let them meet each other's eye
They were not made for one another so don't even try
Cat plus dog equals a fight
If you're not careful they'll quarrel through the night
It's better when you choose between a cat or a dog
If you can't decide then just get a frog
Whichever you choose will settle in your home soon
But if you don't want a cat, dog or frog then try a baboon.

Anne-Marie Mensah

Jaguars

I am the unseen hunter
A shadow of the night
My spots are rarely seen
And when it comes to prey
I always pick a fight.
I stalk like an agent on a mission classified
And when I see the suspect
I take them by surprise.
I frequently patrol the area I've made my home
My fangs are like daggers so don't get too close
'Cause I might be majestic to look at
But I'm not a friendly host
I am the twilight hunter and I bid you adieu.

Danielle Christine Pendlebury (10)

Otis...

W eimar is where this canine's from,
E ven though his hunting's long gone.
I love my dog to the moon and back,
M ajestic and silver with a tinge of black.
A very keen nose with a good sense of smell,
R abbits and squirrels will do him well.
A bit of cheese is his favourite treat,
N ot a stranger are you likely to meet.
E veryone loves Otis, my dog,
R unning away to play with a log.

Olly Bob Kersel (11)

For The Animals

Under the deepest and darkest of sea
Or through the brightest and bluest of skies
On the highest and coldest of mountains
There's a beautiful and magical animal
For you and me.

They live with what Mother Nature has to offer
And are in the wild to be free
Not for us to lock them in cages
Or us to slaughter for our needs and greeds

We all must save the animals
And be their best friends
For there is true beauty in them.

Esha Furrukh (13)

The King Of The Wild

I am a lion,
As strong as iron,
And I can even snap a dandelion,
I am big,
That is why I snap twigs,
My mane is like a wig,
My teeth are sharp knives,
But instead it's in the wildlife,
However, I don't use it to kill my wife,
I am fast,
I never come last,
And a human might end up in a cast,
If you know what I want to eat,
I really, really love my meat,
That's why I tell zebras to meet me at a street,
As I said, I am a lion,
As strong as iron,
And I can even snap a dandelion.

Joshua C Augustine (8)

The Rainbow Unicorn

Rainbow-coloured unicorn
How pretty you are
You travel so far!
Your horn is dazzling bright
On a starry night
You eat fruit and berry delight
Your eyes are as purple as plums
And your ears are as yellow as lemons
I fly you to sweet land
And dance in sugar sand
There are lemonade lakes
And strawberry cakes
Then I get tired and Rainbow does too
As fast as lightning, home to bed
I thank her and pat her on her head.

Sahana Waller (6)

My Lovely Brownie

I have a pet called Brownie
With a twitchy nose
He likes to pose
And he has a wiggly tail
When he plays with his toy snail
When I tickle Brownie's belly
He becomes silly
His spots are white
Like the clouds up high
And when he dances with his paws
I look at him and pause
We go on a walk
And we have a funny talk
When he talks, he barks
When we go to the parks
I love my puppy Brownie
He is my buddy.

Laaiba Haaniya Hassan (7)

Oh I Love Woods!

Oh great, grand owl, your eyes so bright,
Thy hunt and swoop all the night.

Oh stag, your antlers like a twig,
And boar your snout is like a pig's.

Oh badger, your fur is like my pyjamas,
And your soft fluffy coat is like a llama's.

Oh how I love you grizzly bear,
I also love you joyful hare.

Oh scavengers, you search through bins,
But Mr Raccoon there's no food in that tin.

I love you woods, I love you woods,
I love you animals, you're my best buds!

Jared Wright (10)

Why Moths Are My Favourite Insects

Moths aren't fluttery like butterflies,
They are calm and laid back.
They won't snap nor will they trap
They're just searching for light,
And will certainly not start a fight!
Just for this poem,
Imagine if moths are happiness,
And light is emotion
And humans are sadness.
Moths just want to orbit around the light,
But they don't want to be squashed by a sandal
Or hoovered up.
Let's give the moths their true happiness,
Or we'll cause their depression.

Rezwan Islam

Pig On The Run!

A runt of the litter
Not yet though a quitter
With a short pink snout
There was never a doubt
This clever little sausage
Escaped the farm cottage
In search of the shops
For a pail full of slops
But stopped at the fence
For this serious offence
The farmer had wailed
That this pig had failed
His trotters were matching
And his back wanted scratching
As he re-entered the barn
At the bottom of the farm.

Isla Ruddock (7)

A Poem About My Dog, Taran

Taran is a boy
But you couldn't tell by his toy
A bright pink ball
That's always going over the wall.
He loves his treats
That we call doggy sweets.
He loves to go for a ride in the car
And it doesn't matter how far.
When I get out his tinned meat
As fast as light he's there by my feet.
And when I get home from school he covers me in sloppy kisses
That's how I know that it's me Taran misses.

Joshua James Shaw

I Love My Pet

My pet is really special,
I feed her every day.
She may not be a normal pet,
But I love her anyway.

Her skin is soft and scaly,
She's gentle and she's kind.
Her teeth may be a little sharp,
But I don't really mind.

I like to ride upon her back,
Around the local park.
The children all look really scared.
The dogs all start to bark

But they don't see her as I do.
Behind that toothy smile,
She's really such a timid thing,
My lovely crocodile.

Mia Ford (7)

The Harpy Eagle

In the harpy eagle's den,
It is dark, dingy and damp
It is where he lays his head
and reflects evil out of his land
When the harpy eagle swoops down
you jump back in horror!
The harpy eagle owns the sky.
His wings cast a shadow down below.
The harpy eagle is a silent hunter
He takes a power dive to the ground
He creeps up on his prey.
Then as quick as a blink
He vanished... with his prey.

Aidan Edward Ives (9)

What Am I?

I'm swift through sub-saharan Africa,
Chasing for prey to eat tonight.

I have tan-coloured fur
With solid, round, black spots,
So all the animals are friendly to me.

I roam with kindness in my grassy savannah home.

At 8 o'clock at night all the animals pray for the food given
Then at 10 o'clock all the animals fall asleep

Have you guessed what I am?
I am a cheetah!

Het Parmar

Jack Wigglebutt For Sale

Offer today only
One humble wiggling bum dog for sale
Very good at jumping
Often jumps very high
Never gets fed up while wiggling his bum
Brightens your day
Never gives up and never gives in

Very good for warding off enemies
Has toxic breath so don't come near
It's just a cute, funny, smelling, wiggling and soft dog
Don't be scared
He makes you laugh out loud!
To make you even choke
Aww!
So please grab a bargain for the wiggling dog.

Eleazar Obese-Amankwah (9)

Orangutans

Red and orange in the tree.
In the blink of an eye,
They are swinging free and free.

Hair flowing in the breeze,
It's as soft as lace.
If you stare up on a wrinkly branch,
You might just see his happy face.

Orangutans are pretty,
But their manners are a disgrace!
They`re nothing like a kitty,
Who has lots and lots of grace?

But extinction is near for orangutans.
Sad times are coming.
To survive the human threat,
They must be very cunning.

Ella Clark (8)

Animal Changer

From a fox to a lion, even an ox,
This little beast will nibble your socks,
Before you can shove him away,
He alters his shape to a bright blue jay,

He uses his magic to change his form,
Some people say he can even do corn,
As he changes, the colours are blurred,
Human minds can't settle on something so absurd,

I'm the only one who can quieten him now,
He comes bounding to me all meows,
But I know he's just my funny cat Mojo.

Preethi Anbarasan (10)

Cats

Cats, cats, cats,
They snooze all day
And purr out loud like a motorbike engine
Always pounce
They bounce on your lap
A cat will make you feel relaxed
And sleep on your toes
As cosy as a blanket
Like a layer of fluff on top of you
They go away to stretch their legs
Or paws!
But they come back
With a gift
Of a furball
Or a poor sad bird
Or maybe a squeaky mouse!

Lily Steel (7)

Animals' Homes

On top of a mountain peak
Or under the ocean bed
There are millions of places animals can be
In the hot desert where camels live
In a dark cave where bears roam
Or in the jungle where all must be brave
In the wild safari where lions graze
Or in the icy wind of Antarctica
In a tree trunk away from harm
Or inside a hole underneath the ground
There are millions of places animals can be.

Nilesh Saha

Pet Goldfish

G oldfish sparkles like the sun.
O n the beach the goldfish make friends with the jellyfish.
L ittle baby eggs hatching gold.
D epends on if the goldfish is a girl or a boy.
F ish they are all different types of creature.
I n the sea great seahorses are friends with goldfish.
S harks like to eat goldfish.
H orses upon land and horses in the water.

Naomi Ishii Meredith

My Dog

She wags her tail,
She tilts her head,
She barks at squirrels even when she's supposed to be in bed!

She rolls on her belly,
She flashes a smile,
She's still been barking for a while!

She eats her dinner,
She gives a woof,
She sees a treat and she goes poof!

Without my dog,
I don't know what I'd do,
Except for when
She does a poo!

Ria Kaur Kandola

The Playful Panda

There once was a panda,
Small but true,
Black and white,
Like a magpie too.
Always rolling around in lovely plants,
To keep awake he loved to dance.
Right into his mama's arms he came,
Warm and cuddly, tired from his game.
Looking forward to eating food,
Now he's in a hungry mood.
Bamboo branches, bugs that are smelly,
Perfect food for his empty belly,
Go to sleep little one,
Time to rest up and then have some fun.

Matthew Hussey (10)

My Fish

In a magic aqua world
They're gliding fast and free
And in underwater forests
They are hiding secretly.

They're swimming the darkness
And in the shining sun.
Their scales start to shimmer
As they begin to have some fun.

Their colours are like rainbows
As they dance around their land.
Showing off their tails and fins,
So colourful and grand.

Ella Hatch (10)

Little Fish

In the depths of the ocean his fine fins flutter,
Blowing big bubbles while he mutters.
His tiny, beautiful, sharp scales,
Look smoother than the skin of whales!
With his big, blue, beady eyes,
Him and his friends slip through the rocks like spies.
Some are as blue as the sky,
Others tickle me as I swim by.
They all want me to swim with them extremely fast.
Getting more and more tiring I say how long will this last?

Skye Walters

The Cheetah

Cheetah is a fast runner
When it finds prey it is a fast eater
Usually hunts on its own
Sometimes has a friend to help

Cheetahs have padded feet
So it helps to hunt its prey
Cheetahs can't go to Tesco's
And can't have a home delivery
It needs to make its own delivery

Cheetahs don't have TVs or phones
So it needs to entertain on its own.

Mugunth Muthu Ramakrishnan (8)

Kittens

K ittens are very lovely, nice, cool and excellent.
I ndependent, yes, but never inconvenient.
T abbies are very cute, never the slightest bit shabby.
T ypes of kitten are always extremely fabby.
E very life gets better with a few kittens or cats.
N ow you have this poem you know all the facts.
S omething extra for you, always love your cats.

Emily Alice Welbourn (8)

The Lovely Fish

The lovely fish got his dish
And made a very good wish
He switched his TV to mute
And got on with the day
He got a glitch on his fishy phone
And saw what would happen next
That made his wish of a very good fish come true
He went water diving on a surfboard,
Sadly he had to ditch that surfboard of a fish
Later that day he went on a pitch
And found Miss Rich!

Fabian Andrei Hurduc (10)

Vampire Squid

V ery
A ncient
M y friend the squid
P rotected me from a shark one day
I t came to eat me, I shouted, "Help!" and somebody
R escued me. His
E yes were blue. He

S quirted light
Q uickly we hid
U nder his cloak, we turned
I nvisible, we
D isappeared and had tea.

George Lough (7)

The Spotted Hunter

L eopards normally climb trees to eat their prey
E ating gazelles and wildebeest all day
O ver the branches they stay and wait for their prey
P ouncing and using their strong legs and paws
A ttacking deer with their sharp teeth and claws
R unning fast from the forest fires
D estroying their homes
S ave the leopards now!

Annabel Bazire-Smith (6)

I Think

What is that in the trees?
Is it a grey cloud?
Or a koala bear?
I think koala bears
Are very smelly.

What is that on that branch?
Is it a brown pillow?
Or a monkey?
I think monkeys
are very cheeky.

What is that in the river?
Is it a lily pad?
Or an alligator?
I think alligators
Are very snappy.

What is that in the grass?
Is it an orange flower?
Or a tiger?
I think tigers
Are very fierce.

Harry Clark (6)

Snake

I shed my layers of deceit,
In the blistering morning heat.
I lurk in the shadows of the wallowing plains;
Until you are ready for me.
I approach as a small, slithering wreck;
But how mighty I can be.

I wrap up my victim in a blanket of delusion,
Smothering their cries.
Coils upon coils, a cocoon of oppression:
A twisted tale of lies.

Erin Mallon (12)

Come On Baby Animal, Just Who Do You Come From?

Elephants have calves,
Eagles have eaglets,
Lions have cubs,
And snakes have snakelets.

Cats have cute kittens,
Dogs have puppies,
Horses have foals,
And ducks have ducklings.

Butterflies have caterpillars,
Foxes have kits,
Kangaroos have joeys,
And goats have kids.

Welcome animal babies,
Welcome to the fun,
So alike, so different,
But oh! There are so many, can you believe it?

Nicole Cretu (8)

Poachers

Out in the wild where it should be safe
When it goes dark and it gets late
Mean men come and feel that they must
Corner an elephant and take off its tusk
They leave them lying there in a pool of blood
Just because they think ivory is good
They put it in medicine and they use it for jewellery
But this isn't needed and this is just foolery.

Lacie-Mai Wharton (8)

Marvellous Monty

Marvellous Monty lives with me
Cheeky cat, as friendly as can be
Often a wimp and hates the rain
Super smart with a brilliant brain
He likes hiding in cardboard boxes
Terrifies chickens just like foxes!
Silvery stripes, piercing emerald eyes
Overall he's very wise
Foolishly tries to catch bees
Quick learner, keen to please!

Seth Waller (8)

My Turtle, Toffee

This is my turtle,
He lives in a shell,
His name is Toffee
And he likes it very well.
He is a sea turtle,
Green and brown,
He listens to music,
Every night and day,
He has a lot of friends,
His friends are very friendly,
We don't see him much as
He is a sea turtle,
This is my turtle and
He is my friend.

Kenzie-Jay Taylor (10)

Gazelle

G raceful as she glides
A frica's sounds awaken as the sun sets
Z igzag through the brush, higher you leap
E legant and beautiful are your twisted horns and mixed coat colours
L eap higher than you ever have before
L ike the cow who jumped over the moon
E vening has awakened, morning has slept.

Lilli Hayhurst (9)

Chinchillas

They're fluffy,
They're cute,
They're the opposite of mute,
They're black, white, brown,
They never ever frown,
They need a cage, water, food,
They're never in a mood,
They'll always play with you,
They are never sad and blue,
But the best thing about chinchillas is,
They'll always love you!

Ruby Lee (10)

Amazing Animals

Unicorns are high in the sky
If you go on a safari you'll hear the king the kingdom's mighty cry
Sloths are slow, I wonder do they take long to grow?
Whales are kind but dangerous to find.
They can swallow you whole with one small gulp.
In the future this may not be true
The Earth is dying
And needs everyone including you!

Sadie Wise (9)

The Freezing Penguin

Once there was a penguin, very, very freezy,
Waddling through a storm which was very breezy.
The penguin was lonely,
His friends waddling around said he was full of baloney.
He found another penguin sitting on the ice,
The penguin gave him a hug which was warm and nice.
Once there was a penguin, very, very warm,
With another penguin huddling together in the storm.

Eleanor Kate Dang (9)

Storm Wolf

Like a viper, the wolf slowly prowls in amongst the waving reeds
Famished, the aggressive, fuming wolf patrols the hazardous hills
Like a bolt of lightning, the wolf bounds across the stormy terrain
Shredding its wounded prey, like a dog with a newspaper
A cursing howl roams over the swirling mist as midnight strikes
Ears pricked
Jaws drooling
Ready for action.

William Bazire-Smith (9)

The Wildlife

A common house pet, the dog
A man's best friend.
The underground hole maker, the mole
Digs a hole and lives in it.
A safari animal, the giraffe
Tall like most trees.
The tree hugger, the sloth
Lazy and is always hanging off a tree.
The sea's nicest resident, the dolphin
Friendly to all.
The sky's most beautiful, the butterfly
Petite and harmless.

Abby Laidler (17)

Cat

I feel like a cat,
with no name.

I love the hot sun,
and long naps,
and going to nice places.

And I can catch a bird
or a butterfly.

I am a cat
that loves naps
and sleeping in hot places;
like an old log
near a sad, crispy tree.

When I wake up
I will find a nice, happy tree,
Which will smile a big green smile.

I feel like a cat,
and I love the hot sun.

Eboni Summer Charnock (6)

Somewhere Lurks The Buffalo Snake

Somewhere lurks the buffalo snake
Under the grass is his lair
Somewhere lurks the buffalo snake
Beware, beware, beware!
Somewhere lurks the buffalo snake
It jumps out onto its prey
Somewhere lurks the buffalo snake
It might get you today!
So remember, somewhere lurks the buffalo snake
Beware, beware, beware!

Sammy Facey (7)

The Happy Hedgehog

Tiny and cute
Comes out at night
Wears a prickly suit
It might give you a fright!

When the moon shines bright
And there's nothing around
He uses all his might
To find something off the ground.

It's easy to love
It's easy to see
Better than a dove
And something in the sea.

Libby Rose Nelson (9)

All The Animals

I like cats and dogs,
Parrots, tigers, cheetahs and sharks
Lions, giraffes
I'd like a zoo!
Pandas and kangaroos.

There are so many animals, I can't choose...
I love them all so much
Narwhals, bees and even wasps!
I love horses too, their hair and their hooves,
I'd like to have one of my own one day,
To love and ride and play.

Evangeline Rose van Vuuren (5)

The Uni-Leopard

Its horn is purple, its moves are swift,
You need keen eyes because this beauty's quick!

Its coat is silver, its eyes are bronze,
If this animal could talk, it would be never wrong!

They live in caves, big and wide,
Who knows who else lurks inside!

If you have wept for music, for ever so long,
This beautiful beast sings a lovely song!

Molly Varney (9)

Animals

Animals are clever
Animals are smart
Animals can get very close to your heart
I love dogs small or large
I love the way they play and charge
Waggy tails, tongues and bright eyes
Chasing balls, frisbees and sometimes flies!
Then flopping asleep, head on my knees
Always eager to love and happy to please.

Jayden Lloyd Jacques (13)

Snakes

This cobra is deadly
And rules them all
It is the king cobra after all

This snake is the longest of them all
Constricts its prey as tight as a shrinking hole
The python sits on the throne like it is his own

This one lives in the Aussie inland
With one bite costs 300 lives
It's the inland taipan, who bites and you
Will die.

Harrison Bate (10)

I Am An Animal, The Animal Of Me

I am a lion, king of the animals!
I am an eagle, soaring through the skies!
I am a crocodile, snapping my jaws!
I am a bear, snuggling in my cave!
I am a wolf, howling through the night!
I am a gorilla, pounding my chest!
I am a crow, master of the thieves!
I am a rhino, charging bravely!

Whatever I want to be, the animal of me.

Elis Teifi Hallam (9)

My Rabbit

He smells of lavender ever so sweet,
He has a fluffy white tail just like candyfloss,
It makes me want to melt,
His eyes are like chocolate buttons
He prances and leaps and twirls around me,
He hops, he jumps and he skips,
He licks and cuddles but does not bite,
His shiny nose is as bright as the sun,
He is grey, black and white.

Sareena Padayachy (11)

Whale

What's the beautiful song I hear?
Could it be a friendly, wonderful whale?
As quiet as a statue it glides through the water
Like a floating airship, so harmless.
What an elegant, endangered whale!
Slide, glide, float.
What a vast whale.
I see a whale in the wavy, calm, blue, colourful sea.

Iola Welch (7)

Down Behind The Dustbin

Down behind the dustbin,
I met a dog called Molly
Leave me alone!
I'm trying to eat my lolly
Down behind the dustbin
I met Dotty the cat
Go away!
I was chewing a mat.
Down behind the dustbin
I met Jenny the mouse.
"Move away!
I am trying to find a new house!"

Gina Kumar (9)

Friend Or Foe

Claws as sharp as a razor blade,
Ominous in every dark shade.
Eyes as mysterious as the blue moon,
They run away just before noon.

They love to play catch,
Their cuteness has no match.
They have soft fur
And they love to purr!

Cats are vicious,
And also suspicious.
But everyone can agree that they are cute and expeditious!

Anjal Parizad (13)

Animal Riddle

It howls at the moon
I am not referring to a baboon
It is very scary
...and hairy!

Sharp teeth, grey hair...
It could eat you, BEWARE!

When that eerie sound fills the night
It can give you quite a fright.

Can you guess?
I can confess...
It's a wolf!

Adriana Mae Gavazzi (7)

Tune To The Moon

Last night I heard a tune that brought me to the moon,
There was a panda and her name is Amanda.
She was eating bamboo sticks with soda,
She has a friend alligator that was playing the recorder.
It was a great party fiesta with lots of laughter,
But when I woke up the tune was gone and it was noon.

Owen Timothy Dang (7)

Giraffes Are Big...

Giraffes have very long necks.
They are yellow and brown in different patterns.
They swing their necks to keep back the lions and tigers
"I'm not lunch for you today."
They sleep on their feet and eat from the tallest trees.
In case you don't know, they have black tongues.

Darren Johnson (9)

My Cat

My cat's alright,
My cat can make the weirdest sound when he drinks
My cat's alright
My cat thinks he's a dog because when you call him he comes, but only for cuddles
My cat is an amazing cat
I love my cat and you know what?
He loves me
And I know he always will.

Ella Standring (8)

Our Dog, Dobby

Being a puppy he had a cute doggy grin
But over the years he got old and thin
He always loved chasing balls and sticks
Then he'd give us one of his wet soggy licks
Oh how he loved to jump and play
Out in the fields every day
But then he had to pass away
Poor old Dobby.

Elsy Beales (8)

Hamsters Are Cute!

H amsters are sweet and cute
A nd I also have one
M y cat likes to play with him
S weet and cute it's just endless
T hough they are small they're still too cute
E ven my cat likes him, he even
R uns away into our Christmas box!

Isabelle Martin (9)

Cheetah

C heetah, oh cheetah,
H ow do you sprint so fast,
E ven when you are already tired
E ven when you've just run sixty miles (probably)
T he mighty cheetah never gives up
A nd always looks after its cubs
H onestly, they are the best.

Abdou Saho

The Honeybee Poem

Bees hum a beautiful tune
They sing and dance under the moon
They work together to make honey
Which satisfies my tummy

Bees help us pollinate flowers
So they have incredible powers
Bees' numbers are becoming low
So plant flowers to help their numbers grow.

Poppy Ellen Brown (8)

The Rainbow

Little unicorns love playing
They are laughing and having fun
They they see something amazing
It's a rainbow, sparkling in the sun!

Shouting and jumping with joy
They fly over the rainbow
In excitement to reach their toys
So they can play happily all day.

Holly Orrock

Cat

The echoing steps in the middle of the night
The pattering of paws, so soft and light
Otherwise it's pin-drop silence
No one knows of its intelligence
Or its urge to always play
With the mice that are left to decay
No one understands why it's ever so fat
But that's the reason
I am Cat.

Zahira Khan (12)

My Cat Pixie

My cat Pixie is a bit dipsy
She jumps upon my bed
And jumps on my head
I say "Get down!"
But she gives me a big meow
Then off she goes
But she sneaks back and licks my nose
How can I be mad
When she does that?
My big, fluffy, adorable ginger cat.

Ellie-Mae Jeannie Willoughby (11)

Lazy Sloth

Sloth, sloth lying on a tree.
What a lovely view of flowers you see.
Carefully moving for something to eat.
Maybe a little hibiscus leaf?
Sharp claws, clinging to the bark,
Whether it's daytime or whether it's dark.
Sleeping quietly, do not disturb!
Happy dreams little sloth.

Megan Hussey (7)

The Ladybug Poem

L adybugs are farmer's friend
A phids are in trouble when they come near
D anger! A bird hops by
Y ucky fluid oozes from their legs
B ye-bye birdie!
U nder the leaf, they lay their eggs
G ardens are safe - more ladybugs are one the way.

Jasmin Saini (13)

The Leaping Leopard

It sneaks up on its prey
In the middle of the day
Some can be black
So mind your back
It can leap six metres high
And pass a grown adult by
You have to watch out
Its tail will give you a clout
As it is as long as its body
So look out!

Jessica Robyn Darby (7)

Tiger

Tiger, tiger, stalking low
Ears twitch and eyeballs glow
Reddish fur striped with black
Courage, he does not lack.

Apex predator many fear
Especially mice or deer
Beautiful mammal, good swimmer too
If you see one in the wild, lucky you!

Chiara Gavazzi (9)

Tilly

I have a dog called Tilly. She's small, black and white.
She's a big part of our family and she makes our days bright.
She jumps really high, like a bird in the sky.
She runs really fast, through the long grass.
She always likes to bark.
She's a piece of my heart.

Tyler Slater (7)

My Rabbit

I stare into my eyes
And I can see
A rabbit just for me.

Furry, fluffy, scrunchy too
Big, small, medium too
Just the rabbit for me.

Hot, cold, freezing too
Carrots, parsley, dandelion leaves too
Just the rabbit for me.

Mia Barlow (6)

Animyth

D ashing burning flames,
R oars with infuriating fire,
A shes separate into particles,
G ruesomely chews marshmallows, their desire,
O pens its cavern over the Thames,
N ever rudely (or sarcastically) dribbles.

Tayyibah Begum

The Midnight Prowler

Stalking through the field at night,
Predatory gaze to cause a fright,
Claws raked soil and shredded grass,
Paws are sturdy; made to last.

Muscles rippled as it prowled,
Its prey scattered as it growled,
Not the animal you'd expect,
But a tabby... a household pet.

Amy Cook (17)

The Bunny Poem

B unny is fluffy like a pompom cloud.
U seful little lawnmower munching all the grass.
N ervous tiny bunny don't pat it so hard.
N ice little bunny come and have your lunch.
Y our little tail is a cotton ball.

Beatrice Mae Curtis (6)

Dogs Are Helpful

Dogs are great because they give you cuddles
Even though they splash you with wet puddles
They can even help you save your life
Life a fun and happy dancing jive
Dogs are special to me and you
Just don't forget to pick up the poo!

Neive Sarah Homewood (11)

Please Help Snow Leopards

I am spotty
I live in areas which are snowy
I am a snow leopard
Yes, a snow leopard
Please save me, I am dying
Humans are killing and stealing from me
Pollution is stopping me
Some people like me
Help me now!

Taha Ahmad Khan (8)

The Unicorn Pool Party!

This unicorn pool party was not normal,
The pool was full of candy
And the food was so sweet.
The unicorns went crazy,
They went so crazy that they ate the pool.
Hopefully the unicorns are okay.
I hope I come back soon!

Maria Emma Buia

Animals

Lions, tigers, in the breeze
Crocodiles are animals
Dogs say woof!
But don't get scared, they won't bite.
Let's see if you can try to say woof
But watch out
I hope you didn't forget about big Billy the shark!

Jimmy Mower (7)

Snakes

S lithery snakes
N erve-wracking poison
A dders, boa constrictor and python
K illing people is their nature
E very snake is cold-blooded
S till my favourite animal though.

Lydia Evie Voy (9)

What A Dog Likes

A dog likes loves,
And lots of hugs.
A dog likes kisses,
And making wishes.

A dog likes to run
And have lots of fun,
Playing all day in the sun.

A dog likes to bark
And go to the park,
Running around in the streets after dark.

Sophie Jane Heasman (7)

Shadow

S hadow is my kitten's name
H ow the name came, I do not know
A nswering questions
D aily and weekly
O ut of the shadows she prowls meekly
W ondering where she is.

Megan Grove (11)

The Butterfly

I fly high in the sky
I have probably passed you by,
I am an insect so very small,
I have a lifespan of only one year.
This makes me want to shed a tear,
My wings are full of colour,
I am attracted to flowers
I am a butterfly.

Delilah Craig

Dog

D oris the Dalmation did a dance down in Denamrk
O n Oscar the Ori-Pei's 'orribly oversized orange
G rumpy Gretal the great dane growled whilst grimly grinning and growing green groceries.

Grace Lawson

What Animal Am I?

Leaping through the beautiful flowers,
Nibbling on crunchy carrots for hours.
With long ginger ears,
Loud footsteps I can hear
So soft and fluffy
Looking a little scruffy
What am I?

Answer: Bubbles the Bunny.

Aishwarya Kajendran

Giraffe

G reat height
I ncredible neck
R ather graceful
A mazing personality
F ond of each other
F abulous colours of orange and black
E verlasting leaf meal.

Liam Wilson-Cue

Cheetah

C lever cat
H eavy paws
E legant runners
E nergetic and fast
T ough predator
A nxiously looking after their cubs
H ungry hunters with a big appetite.

Skye Hammond

Rainbow Unicorn

All the colours of the world
Mix them up and give them a swirl
I am bright, I am shiny
I'm not a horse or a pony
My name is Willow the rainbocorn
I have special wings and a beautiful horn!

Xaavier Mahmood

Snowflakes

I hop, I hop, I hop
Over the tall bush
I have fluffy skin
With shiny eyes
I love sweet carrots
So I am chubby and cute
I even look like snow
I wonder do you know
Who I am?

Neha Sankaran (5)

Panda

P andas are beautiful
A favourite of mine
N o animal replaces this guy
D o you know that pandas eat bamboo?
A mazing creature of Asia, I hope you'll agree.

Hester Kean (6)

Mickey The Beagle

A dog called Mickey you say,
One scratch at the door awake he came.
You say walkies,
He stamps his feet
Jumps up with joy, breakfast ahoy.
On the sofa he goes to have a long doze.

Elizabeth Lord (9)

The Panda Way

Pandas are black and white
Their eyes are big, green and bright
They like to watch the stars at night
But can you guess who likes to eat bamboo?
Yes that's right, the pandas do!

Jasmine Elizabeth Jane Clarke (8)

The Animals

Bunnies hopping beside the trees
Owls flying where you cannot see
Crocodiles snap in the swamp
Be careful in case they bite you off
Dogs go woof
Cats go meow
Mix them together you will
Make a big row!

Rosie Mower (8)

The Giraffe

I chose a giraffe because they can see us from miles away
The giraffe can see us over his fence
His neck is longer than a tower
The food has lots of fun
By sliding down his neck.

Wilfred Lane-Petter (5)

Ants

Ants, ants everywhere, even in my hair
Ants in my dinner, ants in my tea
Ants why do you want to bother me?
Mummy says no more sugar, she's all in a huff
I think the ants crawled into her bum!

Autumn Joy (7)

Plodo, My Donkey

D onkey, my favourite!
O h my donkey!
N ight-time you always sleep.
K nights protect you
E ek, eek donkey
Y ou are my favourite thing!

Phoevos Konstantinos Galanis (6)

Shark

S idney shark is a winner
H e hunts fish for his dinner
A round the reef Sidney goes
R acing fast he bumps his nose
K ind Sidney lets them go.

James Batson (8)

Mummy Owl

Flying silently
Whoosh...
Swooping down onto a dirty rat
Stop! Don't eat my owlets
Now...
Yum... the owlets eat the rat
Instead of being dinner.

Samuel Griffin (6)

Panda

P eaceful animals
A dventure is what they live for.
N ature's creation
D angers approach their species
A lthough they are harmless.

Isabelle Haines (11)

Harriet

There was once a young hamster called Harriet
She drove her ball like a chariot
Now our lounge is a mess
We must confess
We've had to book in at the Marriott!

Samuel Debenham (8)

Grizzly Bear

Grizzly bear runs
So rare
My grizzly bear has lots of hair
My grizzly bear likes to stare
My grizzly bear loves to glare
My grizzly bear loves me to care.

Charlie West (6)

If I Had A Unicorn

If I had a unicorn I would take it anywhere
She would make me happy
I would tell my daddy
If I had a unicorn I would stay with her
And she would play with me.

Nimrah Jan (10)

The Fox In The Box

Once upon a time there was a great big box
Inside the box was a great big fox
The fox liked playing with stinky socks
Inside his house, the great big box.

Ieuan Ellis Bridge (5)

Elephants!

Elephants are super big
Elephants' eyes are super small
Elephants' feet can break a twig
Elephants' bodies are the biggest of all.

Evelyn Jane Reilly (10)

Unicorns

Unicorns are so unique
In a magical land where you will seek
You'll see a whole herd of them
As unique as can be
Unicorns rule!

Isla Pacey (11)

Playtime In The Jungle

A baby sloth plays with his pet moth
A macaw waves its teddy's paw
An orangutan sang
A snake made a mud cake.

Phoenix Brooklyn-Lusted (6)

Leo And Miss Miggins The Cat

Leo loves Miss Miggins
I like to stroke her head
When she climbs upon my bed.

Leonardo Fortino (5)

My Dog

A haiku

My dog's furry cute
A super support of love
Funny and clever.

Jake S (13)

Samson

As dark as the night
As warm as the sun
A cuddly dog,
My Samson.

Annabelle Daisy Craig

Puffin

A haiku

Stripy colours pop
As I plunge into the sea
Hunting for my tea.

Noa Bendita Wilkes (9)

Young Writers Information

We hope you have enjoyed reading this book – and that you will continue to in the coming years.

If you're a young writer who enjoys reading and creative writing, or the parent of an enthusiastic poet or story writer, do visit our website **www.youngwriters.co.uk**. Here you will find free competitions, workshops and games, as well as recommended reads, a poetry glossary and our blog. There's lots to keep budding writers motivated to write!

If you would like to order further copies of this book, or any of our other titles, then please give us a call or order via your online account.

Young Writers
Remus House
Coltsfoot Drive
Peterborough
PE2 9BF
(01733) 890066
info@youngwriters.co.uk

Join in the conversation!
Tips, news, giveaways and much more!

YoungWritersUK   @YoungWritersCW